Hall of opulence and mirrors
Versailles, France (opposite page)

Images from Atwood

Chandeliers and Round Things

Chandeliers and Round Things

Images from Atwood

For artisans and friends

Copyright 2016, Echo Hill Arts Press, LLC
All rights reserved, including the right to
reproduce any part of this book.
ISBN: 13-978-1534960428
Colorado Springs, CO, USA

Antique light fixture at Edison-Ford winter compound Fort Myers, Florida (Shown upside down, just for fun)

Unfinished Sagrada Familia Barcelona, Spain

Rarified ceiling

Artichoke flower with bees

Notre Dame, Paris France

Apricot salad and hummus

Ceiling chandelier in the main lodge, Grand Canyon, North Rim

Water garden one

Water garden two

Reflection in bathroom mirror

Oil drop on a wet road

Ceiling light diffuser

Sunlight diffuser

Pulling out of the terminal

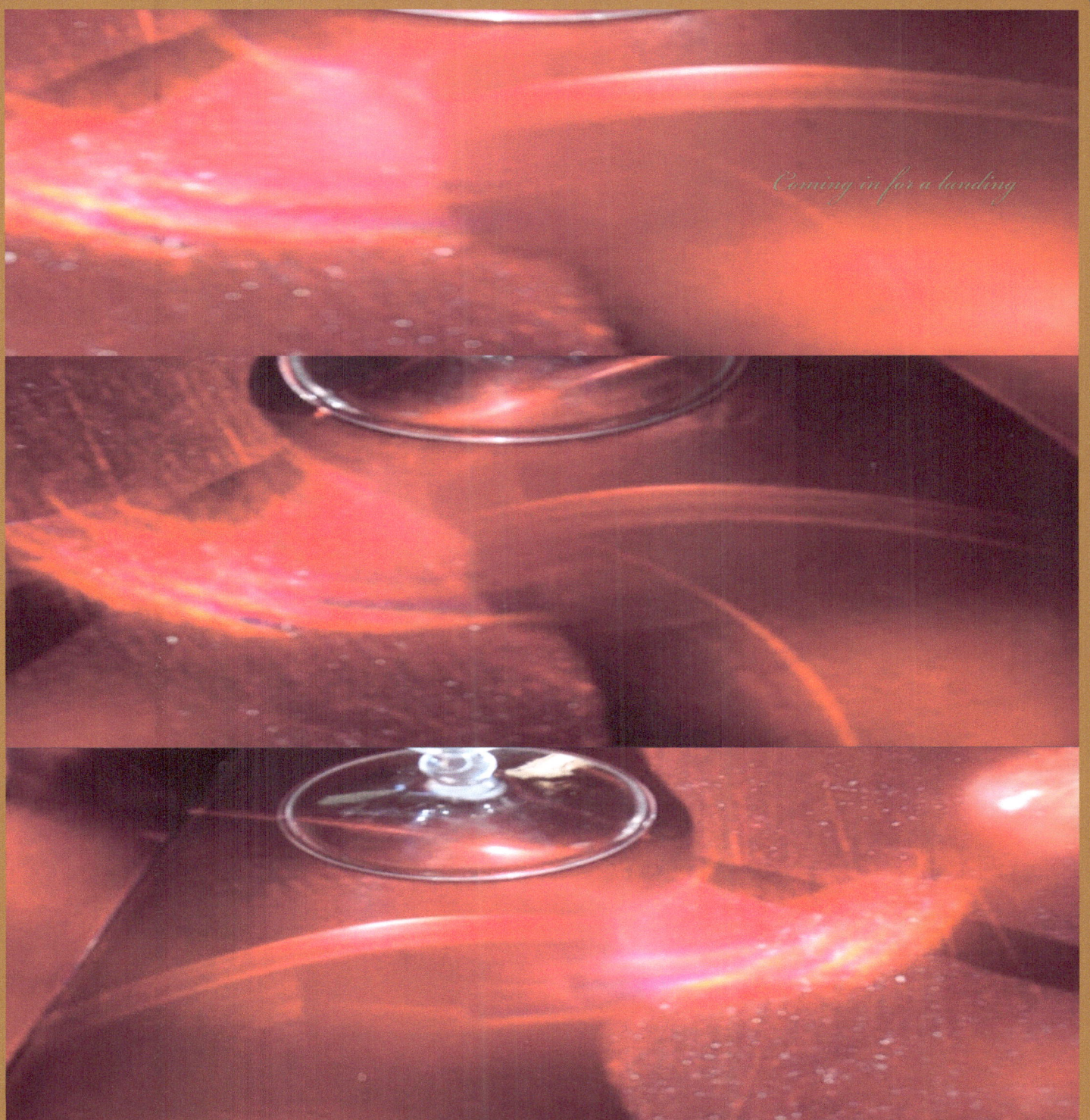

All aglow in the night

Miniature tree-scape

The beginning of a braided rug

Platter for sale, Santa Fe, New Mexico

Dinner at Adena's

Echo Hill Arts
is pleased to make a new line of
Images from Atwood
Photographic Diversions for Areas of Waiting

available Print on Demand
through **Amazon.com** *and* **CreateSpace Direct**

Echo Hill Arts Press